K. CONNORS

Ulysses S. Grant Biography

The Untold Story of America's Most Determined General and Resilient President

Copyright © 2024 by K. Connors

All rights reserved. No part of this publication may be reproduced, stored or transmitted in any form or by any means, electronic, mechanical, photocopying, recording, scanning, or otherwise without written permission from the publisher. It is illegal to copy this book, post it to a website, or distribute it by any other means without permission.

First edition

This book was professionally typeset on Reedsy. Find out more at reedsy.com

Contents

Introduction: Setting the Stage for Ulysses S. Grant's...   1
Chapter 1: Early Life and Background   4
Chapter 2: Military Beginnings   8
Chapter 3: The Civil War Begins   13
Chapter 4: Turning the Tide   18
Chapter 5: Commanding General   23
Chapter 6: The Road to Appomattox   28
Chapter 7: Post-War Challenges   32
Chapter 8: Presidency   37
Chapter 9: Later Years   42
Chapter 10: Legacy and Impact   46
Conclusion: Reflections on Ulysses S. Grant's Journey   50

Introduction: Setting the Stage for Ulysses S. Grant's Remarkable Journey

Understanding the life of Ulysses S. Grant means delving into a story filled with unexpected turns, perseverance, and remarkable transformations. This biography aims to provide a comprehensive look at Grant's life, from his modest beginnings to his pivotal role in American history. Whether you're familiar with his legacy or just curious about this historical figure, you're in for an engaging journey through the 19th century.

Grant was a man of many contradictions: a quiet individual who became a decisive leader, a military genius who despised war's brutality, and a president who fought for civil rights but was marred by scandals. Born as Hiram Ulysses Grant in Ohio, his name was changed due to a clerical error at West Point, thus creating Ulysses S. Grant. This mix-up was a fitting start for a man whose life would be defined by overcoming adversity and embracing the unexpected.

Picture mid-19th century America, a nation rife with tension over slavery, states' rights, and economic disparity. Into this volatile environment stepped Grant, who, despite showing little initial ambition, would leave a lasting mark on history. His early years were unremarkable, more focused on farming and a love for horses than on any grand aspirations of leadership. Yet, life has a way of steering us where we need to go, even if we don't realize it at the time.

Grant's stint at West Point was less than stellar; he graduated in the middle of his class, a rather unremarkable start for someone who would later command the Union Army. But here's a nugget of wisdom: greatness isn't always apparent from the outset. Grant's early military career took him to the Mexican-American War, where he gained vital experience and developed a complex view of warfare.

When the Civil War erupted, Grant, initially struggling to secure a commission, found his stride. He quickly rose through the ranks, demonstrating his strategic acumen in battles like Vicksburg and Shiloh. These victories weren't just military successes; they were crucial turning points in the war that showcased Grant's leadership and resilience. His approach was straightforward and unpretentious, focusing on leading by example rather than grandstanding.

One of Grant's defining moments came at Appomattox Court House, where he negotiated the surrender of Robert E. Lee's army, effectively ending the Civil War. This act not only cemented his place in history but also demonstrated his commitment to reconciliation and peace. As the war ended, the nation faced the daunting task of reconstruction, and Grant's role in this period was both significant and controversial.

Grant's presidency, often overshadowed by scandals like the Whiskey Ring and the Panic of 1873, was a mixed bag. He championed civil rights, fighting against the Ku Klux Klan and working to rebuild the South, but his administration was also marked by corruption and economic challenges. It's a reminder that leadership is fraught with complexities and that even well-intentioned efforts can be marred by unforeseen difficulties.

In his post-presidential years, Grant experienced a whirlwind of triumphs and trials. Celebrated on a world tour and then faced with financial ruin, Grant's later life was a testament to his resilience. Battling terminal cancer, he penned his memoirs, securing his family's financial future and leaving a literary masterpiece. His memoirs remain a classic, reflecting his unflinching honesty and indomitable spirit.

As we dive into the chapters of this biography, we'll explore the pivotal moments of Grant's life, from the muddy battlefields to the White House's grandeur, and from the peaks of success to the depths of personal struggle. Each chapter will not only recount historical events but also draw out lessons and insights that resonate today.

This is not just a recounting of dates and battles; it's an exploration of the human spirit's capacity for resilience, transformation, and redemption. Ulysses S. Grant's life is a rich tapestry of triumph and tragedy, ambition and humility, making him a figure worth understanding deeply. So, as we embark on this journey through his life, prepare to see history through a lens that is both informative and engaging, shedding new light on a man who played a pivotal role in shaping the nation.

Let's begin this exploration of Ulysses S. Grant, a man whose legacy continues to influence and inspire.

Chapter 1: Early Life and Background

Ulysses S. Grant's story begins in a small, unassuming town in Ohio, a far cry from the grandeur and power he would later wield as a general and president. Born Hiram Ulysses Grant on April 27, 1822, in Point Pleasant, Ohio, his early life set the stage for the values and work ethic that would define his character. Grant's childhood was not marked by extraordinary events, but rather by the simplicity and routine of rural life in the early 19th century.

Grant was the first of six children born to Jesse and Hannah Grant. Jesse Grant was a tanner and a businessman, a hardworking man who expected the same diligence from his children. The tanning business, which involved the processing of animal hides into leather, was grueling and smelly work, and young Ulysses was not particularly fond of it. In fact, he often went to great lengths to avoid the tannery, preferring instead to spend his time outdoors, especially with horses.

Horses were Grant's true passion. From a young age, he showed an exceptional talent for handling and riding them. Whether it was plowing fields, transporting goods, or racing, Grant was happiest when he was with horses. This skill would later serve him well in his military career, where the ability to manage cavalry and understand logistics would be crucial.

Despite his father's ambitions for him, Grant did not have grand plans. He was an average student, more interested in daydreaming and outdoor activities than in academics. This lack of academic fervor led Jesse to seek a more structured environment for his son, one that would hopefully instill some discipline and direction. Thus, in 1839, Jesse secured Ulysses an appointment to the United States Military Academy at West Point. There was just one small hitch: a clerical error on his application changed his name from Hiram Ulysses to Ulysses S. Grant, a name that would become legendary.

Grant's time at West Point was unremarkable. He was not an exemplary student by any means, often struggling with the rigorous academic and military curriculum. He graduated 21st in a class of 39, a middle-of-the-road performance that hinted at neither the failures nor the successes that lay ahead. Grant's years at West Point, however, were not without their highlights. He developed close friendships and a reputation for being honest and straightforward—traits that would serve him well throughout his life.

One of the most significant aspects of Grant's West Point experience was his exposure to a diverse group of cadets from different parts of the country. This exposure broadened his horizons and gave him a deeper understanding of the regional tensions simmering in the United States. It was also at West Point that Grant first demonstrated his exceptional skill with horses, earning the admiration of his peers for his ability to ride and manage even the most difficult mounts.

After graduating from West Point in 1843, Grant was assigned to the 4th Infantry Regiment and stationed at various posts. His early military career was relatively uneventful until the outbreak of the Mexican-American War in 1846. During this conflict, Grant served under General Zachary Taylor and later under General Winfield Scott. The war was a formative experience for Grant. He saw combat for the first time and exhibited bravery and competence, earning brevet promotions for his actions at the Battles of Resaca de la Palma and Monterey.

The Mexican-American War also provided Grant with invaluable lessons in leadership and strategy. He observed the strengths and weaknesses of his commanding officers, learning what to emulate and what to avoid. Additionally, Grant's firsthand experiences with the horrors of war deepened his aversion to conflict, a sentiment that would influence his later decisions as a military leader and president.

After the war, Grant returned to a series of peacetime assignments, many of which were mundane and unfulfilling. These years were challenging for Grant, both professionally and personally. In 1848, he married Julia Dent, the sister of a West Point classmate. The couple's deep affection for each other would be a cornerstone of Grant's life, providing him with emotional support through the many trials he would face.

Grant's post-war military assignments took him to remote postings, including a stint in California during the Gold Rush. These assignments were marred by loneliness and homesickness, exacerbated by the distance from his family. It was during this period that Grant's struggles with alcohol began to surface. Isolated and unhappy, he turned to drinking as a way to cope with his frustrations and the tedium of his duties. His drinking would become a recurring issue, affecting his reputation and career.

In 1854, disillusioned and struggling with his alcoholism, Grant resigned from the army. He returned to civilian life, attempting to make a living through various ventures, including farming and real estate, but with little success. The years following his resignation were marked by financial difficulties and a sense of aimlessness. Grant's farming efforts, in particular, were hampered by his lack of enthusiasm and experience in the field. It seemed that nothing he tried could lift him out of the financial instability that plagued him.

Despite these setbacks, Grant's unwavering determination and resilience kept him going. He refused to give up, continuing to search for a way to support his family. This period of hardship would later inform his deep empathy for ordinary Americans struggling to make ends meet, an empathy that would influence his policies as president.

By 1860, Grant had moved his family back to Galena, Illinois, where he worked in his father's leather goods store. It was a humbling position for a former officer, but Grant approached it with the same diligence he had applied to every task. Little did he know that his fortunes were about to change dramatically.

As the nation moved closer to civil war, Grant's military experience and leadership skills would soon thrust him back into the public eye. The quiet years in Galena were merely the calm before the storm that would propel Ulysses S. Grant into the annals of history.

Grant's early life and background are a testament to the power of perseverance and the unexpected twists that life can take. From a modest upbringing and a series of unremarkable early career moves, he rose to become one of the most significant figures in American history. His journey reminds us that greatness often emerges from the most unlikely beginnings and that every setback can be a stepping stone to future success.

Chapter 2: Military Beginnings

After graduating from West Point, Ulysses S. Grant was commissioned as a brevet second lieutenant in the 4th Infantry Regiment. The military life was not what Grant had envisioned for himself, but he took his duties seriously, if somewhat reluctantly. His first assignments were relatively uneventful, involving the typical routines of a peacetime army. However, these early experiences laid the groundwork for his later military success.

Grant's first posting was in the Jefferson Barracks near St. Louis, Missouri. This assignment allowed him to stay close to Julia Dent, whom he had met and fallen in love with while at West Point. The proximity to Julia was a silver lining in an otherwise mundane duty. The young couple's courtship blossomed, and they were married in 1848. Julia's support and love would become a bedrock for Grant throughout his life, especially during the challenging times ahead.

In 1844, Grant's regiment was moved to the Red River region of Louisiana. It was here that he began to experience the harsh realities of military life. The swamps and heat were oppressive, and the monotony of garrison duty weighed heavily on him. Grant found solace in his comrades and his ever-growing love for horses. Despite the tedium, he performed his duties with diligence and a sense of responsibility that his superiors noted, if not overly praised.

The real turning point in Grant's early military career came with the outbreak of the Mexican-American War in 1846. The conflict began over territorial

CHAPTER 2: MILITARY BEGINNINGS

disputes following the annexation of Texas, and Grant's regiment was ordered to join General Zachary Taylor's Army of Occupation in Texas. For the first time, Grant found himself on the move and in a position where his actions would have significant consequences.

Grant's baptism by fire came at the Battle of Palo Alto on May 8, 1846. He was in charge of a supply train and witnessed the chaos and carnage of battle firsthand. Despite the fear and confusion, Grant remained composed and carried out his duties effectively. This early exposure to combat taught him the importance of calm under pressure, a trait that would define his later leadership.

Following Palo Alto, Grant participated in several key battles, including Resaca de la Palma and Monterey. At Resaca de la Palma, he demonstrated remarkable bravery by volunteering for a dangerous mission to retrieve a cannon that had been left behind in no-man's-land. Grant and a few comrades successfully completed the mission under heavy fire, earning him a reputation for courage and quick thinking.

One of Grant's most notable actions during the Mexican-American War occurred at the Battle of Monterey. During a lull in the fighting, Grant's unit found itself pinned down by enemy fire. Seizing an opportunity, Grant mounted a horse and rode through the streets under intense fire to deliver orders. This daring maneuver not only succeeded but also boosted the morale of his fellow soldiers. Acts like this one showcased Grant's willingness to take risks and his innate leadership qualities.

Grant's service under General Winfield Scott in the campaign to capture Mexico City further honed his military skills. He participated in the battles of Molino del Rey and Chapultepec, where he continued to distinguish himself. At Chapultepec, Grant once again demonstrated his courage by carrying a dispatch across a battlefield under heavy fire, using a disassembled howitzer carriage for cover. This clever improvisation not only highlighted his resourcefulness but also his commitment to the mission.

The Mexican-American War had a profound impact on Grant. He witnessed the horrors of war up close and developed a deep respect for the discipline and bravery of soldiers. However, he also became critical of the political motivations behind the conflict. In his memoirs, Grant later described the war as "one of the most unjust ever waged by a stronger against a weaker nation." This perspective would influence his views on conflict and diplomacy in the years to come.

After the war, Grant returned to a series of peacetime assignments, many of which he found mundane and unfulfilling. His postings included stints at remote forts in Michigan and California. These assignments were far from the action and excitement he had experienced in Mexico, and they left Grant feeling restless and disillusioned. It was during this time that his struggles with alcohol began to surface more prominently. Isolated and unhappy, Grant turned to drinking as a way to cope with the monotony and loneliness of frontier life.

Grant's assignment to Fort Vancouver in the Oregon Territory was particularly challenging. The remote location and harsh conditions took a toll on his morale. Despite his best efforts to stay focused on his duties, the isolation exacerbated his drinking problem. Recognizing the detrimental impact this was having on his career, Grant made several attempts to curb his drinking, but with mixed success.

In 1854, facing mounting pressure and disillusioned with his military prospects, Grant resigned from the army. He returned to civilian life, hoping to find stability and purpose outside the military. This transition was far from smooth. Grant struggled to find his footing in various ventures, including farming and real estate, but with limited success. His financial difficulties and a sense of failure weighed heavily on him during these years.

CHAPTER 2: MILITARY BEGINNINGS

Grant's post-military life was marked by a series of challenges and setbacks. His attempts at farming near St. Louis were largely unsuccessful, partly due to his lack of enthusiasm for the work and partly due to bad luck. Grant's farming venture, which he called "Hardscrabble," lived up to its name, leaving him with more debts than profits. Despite these hardships, Grant's determination and resilience kept him going. He refused to give up, continuing to search for ways to support his family.

By 1860, Grant had moved his family to Galena, Illinois, where he worked in his father's leather goods store. It was a humbling position for a former officer, but Grant approached it with the same diligence he had applied to every task. Little did he know that his fortunes were about to change dramatically with the outbreak of the Civil War.

Grant's early military career was a rollercoaster of experiences, from the highs of battlefield bravery to the lows of peacetime monotony and personal struggles. These formative years were crucial in shaping his character and leadership style. The lessons learned and the challenges faced during this period would prepare him for the immense responsibilities and trials that awaited him during the Civil War and beyond.

In reflecting on Grant's military beginnings, one can see the seeds of his later greatness. His courage, resourcefulness, and unwavering commitment to duty were evident even in his earliest assignments. While his path was far from smooth, each twist and turn added to the depth and resilience of the man who would one day lead the Union Army to victory and guide a nation through its post-war recovery.

Grant's story is a testament to the idea that true leadership is forged in the crucible of experience, both good and bad. His early military career, with its mix of triumphs and tribulations, set the stage for the remarkable achievements that would define his legacy. As we move forward in this biography, we will see how these early experiences laid the foundation for

Grant's rise to prominence and his enduring impact on American history.

Chapter 3: The Civil War Begins

By 1861, the United States was on the brink of an internal cataclysm. The issue of slavery had divided the nation deeply, and the secession of Southern states marked the beginning of the Civil War. Ulysses S. Grant, then living a modest life in Galena, Illinois, working at his father's leather goods store, was about to step back into the military spotlight in a way that would alter the course of American history.

When the first shots were fired at Fort Sumter in April 1861, the country was thrust into chaos. The call to arms resonated across the nation, and like many former soldiers, Grant felt a duty to serve. Although he had struggled in civilian life and faced personal challenges, the onset of war provided a new sense of purpose. He immediately began organizing a company of volunteers in Galena, demonstrating his natural leadership and organizational skills.

Grant's initial attempts to rejoin the military were not without hurdles. His past resignation from the army and struggles with alcohol had left him with a less-than-stellar reputation. However, his persistence paid off, and he was eventually appointed as a colonel of the 21st Illinois Volunteer Infantry Regiment. This appointment marked the beginning of Grant's remarkable ascent through the ranks.

The first significant challenge for Grant and his regiment was the task of transforming a group of raw recruits into a disciplined fighting force. The

21st Illinois was a motley crew, full of enthusiasm but lacking in military experience. Grant's experience and no-nonsense attitude were crucial in molding these men into a cohesive unit. He emphasized discipline, training, and preparation, ensuring his troops were ready for the rigors of war.

Grant's early engagements in the Civil War set the tone for his leadership style and strategic approach. His first notable action was the seizure of Paducah, Kentucky, in September 1861. This small but strategically important town controlled access to key rivers, and its capture was a significant early victory for the Union. Grant's decisiveness and ability to act swiftly were on full display, earning him recognition and setting the stage for larger commands.

Following the success at Paducah, Grant was promoted to brigadier general, thanks in part to the influence of his political connections, including Congressman Elihu B. Washburne, who was a staunch supporter. Grant's promotion came at a time when the Union desperately needed effective leaders. The war was escalating, and both sides were gearing up for major conflicts.

One of Grant's first major battles as a brigadier general was the Battle of Belmont in November 1861. The engagement was a mixed bag—a tactical success but a strategic retreat. Grant aimed to disrupt Confederate forces and supply lines near the Mississippi River, and his forces managed to inflict significant damage. However, the battle also highlighted the chaos and unpredictability of war. Grant himself narrowly escaped capture, demonstrating both his bravery and the razor-thin margins between victory and disaster.

The experience at Belmont was a valuable learning opportunity for Grant. He realized the importance of maintaining the initiative and the psychological impact of bold action. Despite the mixed results, Grant's superiors recognized his potential, and he continued to rise through the ranks, gaining command of the District of Southeast Missouri.

It was in early 1862 that Grant's true military genius began to shine. The campaign to capture Forts Henry and Donelson in Tennessee marked his first major victories and solidified his reputation as a tenacious and effective commander. The capture of these forts was crucial for the Union's strategy to control the Western theater of the war. Fort Henry fell relatively easily in February 1862, thanks to the cooperation between Grant's ground forces and the Union navy.

Fort Donelson, however, was a different story. This fortress was well-defended and strategically significant, sitting on the Cumberland River. The battle for Fort Donelson was intense, involving fierce fighting in harsh winter conditions. Grant's leadership during this engagement was exemplary. He coordinated a combined assault with naval forces, demonstrating his ability to integrate different branches of the military effectively.

The turning point came when Grant demanded the "unconditional and immediate surrender" of the Confederate forces at Fort Donelson. This bold demand not only led to the surrender of approximately 12,000 Confederate troops but also earned Grant the nickname "Unconditional Surrender" Grant. The victory was a significant morale booster for the Union and a severe blow to the Confederacy. It also catapulted Grant into the national spotlight, making him one of the Union's most celebrated generals.

The success at Fort Donelson was followed by the Battle of Shiloh in April 1862, one of the bloodiest battles in American history up to that point. The battle was a brutal awakening for both sides, revealing the true horror and scale of the Civil War. Grant's forces were surprised by a Confederate attack at dawn, and the first day saw the Union troops pushed back significantly.

Despite the initial setbacks, Grant's determination and refusal to retreat turned the tide. He regrouped his forces, and with reinforcements arriving, launched a counterattack on the second day. The Union forces managed to regain lost ground and ultimately forced the Confederate army to withdraw. The Battle of Shiloh was a strategic victory for the Union, but it came at a tremendous cost, with thousands of casualties on both sides.

Shiloh was a sobering experience for Grant. It taught him the importance of preparedness and the brutal realities of warfare. The heavy casualties drew criticism from many quarters, and some even called for his removal. However, President Abraham Lincoln famously defended Grant, saying, "I can't spare this man; he fights." Lincoln's support was crucial, allowing Grant to continue his command and learn from the experience.

As the Civil War continued, Grant's role expanded. He was given command of the Army of the Tennessee and tasked with leading the Union efforts in the Western Theater. His focus turned to Vicksburg, Mississippi, a fortress city that was key to controlling the Mississippi River. The Vicksburg campaign would become one of Grant's most significant achievements, demonstrating his strategic brilliance and relentless determination.

Grant's approach to Vicksburg involved a series of maneuvers and battles aimed at isolating the city. He cut off supply lines, engaged in battles at places like Champion Hill and Big Black River, and finally laid siege to Vicksburg. The siege lasted for several weeks, with Union forces gradually tightening their grip around the city. On July 4, 1863, Vicksburg surrendered, giving the Union control of the Mississippi River and splitting the Confederacy in two.

The fall of Vicksburg was a turning point in the Civil War, cementing Grant's reputation as one of the Union's most effective generals. It also showcased his ability to conduct large-scale operations and his understanding of the broader strategic picture. Grant's success at Vicksburg earned him a promotion to major general in the regular army and set the stage for his future leadership roles.

Grant's early experiences in the Civil War were a mix of challenges and triumphs, each contributing to his growth as a military leader. His ability to learn from mistakes, his strategic insight, and his unyielding determination were key factors in his rise. The early battles and campaigns not only tested his mettle but also prepared him for the monumental tasks that lay ahead.

In reflecting on the beginning of Grant's Civil War career, one can see the qualities that would define his leadership: boldness, resilience, and an unwavering commitment to victory. These attributes would propel him through the war's darkest days and ultimately lead to the Union's triumph. As we continue this journey through Grant's life, we will see how these early experiences shaped him into the leader who would help reunite a divided nation and leave an indelible mark on American history.

Chapter 4: Turning the Tide

By 1863, Ulysses S. Grant had already established himself as a formidable force in the Union Army. The successes at Fort Donelson and the bloody endurance test of Shiloh had proven his resilience and strategic acumen. But it was the Vicksburg Campaign that would truly showcase Grant's military genius and cement his reputation as a pivotal figure in the Civil War. This chapter delves into how Grant turned the tide of the war, emphasizing his leadership during critical battles and his unique approach to warfare.

The city of Vicksburg, Mississippi, was a strategic linchpin for the Confederacy. Perched high on bluffs overlooking the Mississippi River, it controlled the crucial supply lines and split the Confederacy in two. Capturing Vicksburg would give the Union control of the river, effectively bisecting the Confederate states and strangling their resources. It was a high-stakes target, and Grant was determined to seize it.

Grant's approach to the Vicksburg Campaign was a masterclass in military strategy and perseverance. He faced numerous challenges, not least of which was the difficult terrain and the strong Confederate defenses. Early attempts to bypass Vicksburg's defenses by digging canals and navigating the swamps met with limited success and plenty of frustrations. These setbacks could have demoralized a lesser commander, but Grant remained undeterred, adapting his strategies with each failure.

CHAPTER 4: TURNING THE TIDE

In the spring of 1863, Grant launched a daring plan to move his troops south of Vicksburg, cross the Mississippi River, and attack the city from the east. This maneuver involved a risky and arduous march through the swamps and bayous of Louisiana, a testament to Grant's willingness to take bold risks. He coordinated with Admiral David Dixon Porter's naval forces to run past the Vicksburg batteries under the cover of darkness, a move that required nerves of steel and precise timing.

Grant's audacity paid off. By late April, his forces had crossed the river and were positioned to strike. The subsequent campaign was a whirlwind of battles and rapid movements, designed to confuse and outmaneuver the Confederate defenders. In a span of just a few weeks, Grant's army won a series of crucial engagements, including the battles of Port Gibson, Raymond, Jackson, Champion Hill, and Big Black River Bridge. These victories effectively cut off Vicksburg from reinforcements and supplies.

One of the most striking aspects of Grant's leadership during the Vicksburg Campaign was his ability to maintain momentum and pressure. Unlike many of his contemporaries who often hesitated after initial successes, Grant kept pushing forward, understanding that relentless pressure would eventually break the enemy. His determination to maintain the initiative and keep Confederate forces off balance was a key factor in the campaign's success.

By late May 1863, Grant had encircled Vicksburg and began a siege that would last for 47 days. The conditions for the defenders were dire. Cut off from supplies and under constant bombardment, the Confederate soldiers and civilians in Vicksburg endured tremendous hardships. Food became scarce, and residents were forced to live in caves dug into the hillsides to escape the shelling. Grant's forces tightened the noose, methodically digging trenches and advancing their lines closer to the city's fortifications.

The siege of Vicksburg was not just a military operation; it was a psychological battle as well. Grant's tactics and the relentless Union bombardment wore down the defenders' will to fight. On July 4, 1863, Confederate General John C. Pemberton surrendered Vicksburg to Grant. The fall of Vicksburg was a devastating blow to the Confederacy and a turning point in the war. The Union now controlled the Mississippi River, effectively splitting the Confederate states and cutting off vital supply lines.

Grant's triumph at Vicksburg had far-reaching implications. It boosted Union morale and solidified Grant's reputation as a leading general. President Abraham Lincoln recognized the significance of the victory, famously remarking, "The Father of Waters again goes unvexed to the sea." This victory, coupled with the Union success at Gettysburg, which occurred almost simultaneously, marked a decisive shift in the war's momentum in favor of the North.

Following the Vicksburg Campaign, Grant was promoted to major general in the regular army, a reflection of his growing stature and the confidence placed in him by Union leadership. His next challenge was the Chattanooga Campaign, where he would again demonstrate his strategic brilliance and ability to inspire his troops.

The Battle of Chattanooga, fought in November 1863, was another critical engagement. The Union forces, under siege by Confederate troops, were in a precarious position. Grant arrived and quickly set to work, revitalizing the demoralized Union soldiers and planning a series of bold maneuvers to break the siege. His ability to inspire confidence and instill discipline in his troops was instrumental in the eventual Union victory.

One of the most dramatic moments of the Chattanooga Campaign was the assault on Lookout Mountain, often referred to as the "Battle Above the Clouds." Union forces, under the command of Major General Joseph Hooker, scaled the steep and fog-covered slopes, driving the Confederates from their positions. This audacious attack, combined with a successful assault on Missionary Ridge, forced the Confederate army to retreat and lifted the siege of Chattanooga.

CHAPTER 4: TURNING THE TIDE

Grant's victories at Vicksburg and Chattanooga cemented his reputation as a decisive and effective leader. These campaigns showcased his ability to execute complex operations, adapt to changing circumstances, and maintain relentless pressure on the enemy. They also highlighted his talent for inspiring his troops and getting the best out of his subordinates.

Grant's leadership style was characterized by a blend of pragmatism and boldness. He was not one for grandiose statements or flashy displays; instead, he focused on clear objectives and straightforward plans. His calm demeanor under pressure and his willingness to take calculated risks earned him the respect and loyalty of his men. Grant's ability to learn from his experiences and adapt his strategies was a key factor in his success.

As 1864 dawned, Grant's successes had not gone unnoticed by President Lincoln and the Union high command. The war was far from over, and the Union needed a leader who could bring it to a successful conclusion. In March 1864, Grant was promoted to the rank of lieutenant general and given command of all Union armies, a position previously held only by George Washington.

Grant's new role marked a significant shift in the Union's strategy. He developed a coordinated plan to apply simultaneous pressure on multiple fronts, aiming to stretch the Confederate forces to their breaking point. His focus was on aggressive action and leveraging the Union's superior resources to wear down the Confederacy. This strategy would lead to some of the war's most intense and bloody battles, but it was a necessary approach to achieve ultimate victory.

Grant's tenure as general-in-chief was marked by his partnership with Major General William Tecumseh Sherman. The two men shared a similar vision and strategic mindset, allowing them to work effectively together. While Grant focused on the Eastern Theater and his direct confrontation with General Robert E. Lee, Sherman embarked on his famous March to the Sea, cutting a swath through the South and further crippling the Confederate war effort.

Grant's ability to coordinate and oversee complex operations across multiple theaters demonstrated his strategic genius and administrative acumen. He understood the importance of logistics, the need for relentless pressure, and the psychological aspects of warfare. His leadership during this period was crucial in bringing the Civil War to a close and setting the stage for the reunification of the nation.

In summary, the period from 1863 to early 1864 was pivotal for Ulysses S. Grant and the Union Army. Grant's victories at Vicksburg and Chattanooga turned the tide of the war and demonstrated his exceptional leadership and strategic abilities. These campaigns showcased his willingness to take risks, his capacity to inspire and lead his troops, and his skill in executing complex military operations. As he assumed command of all Union forces, Grant's vision and determination would play a crucial role in the final chapters of the Civil War, leading to the eventual surrender of the Confederate forces and the preservation of the United States.

Chapter 5: Commanding General

By the spring of 1864, Ulysses S. Grant had earned his stripes as a military leader who not only achieved victories but also understood the bigger picture of warfare. His promotion to lieutenant general and command of all Union armies was a testament to his skill, determination, and the confidence placed in him by President Abraham Lincoln. Now, with the weight of the entire Union war effort on his shoulders, Grant was about to face his most daunting challenge yet: bringing the Civil War to a decisive end.

Grant's elevation to the role of Commanding General marked a significant shift in Union strategy. Up to this point, the Union forces had operated somewhat independently, lacking coordination and a unified approach. Grant's first order of business was to change that. He developed a comprehensive plan to synchronize the efforts of all Union armies, ensuring that they would strike simultaneously and prevent the Confederates from shifting their forces to reinforce different fronts. This strategy was designed to stretch the Confederacy's already strained resources and force them into a defensive posture.

One of the first and most crucial components of Grant's strategy was his decision to take personal command of the Army of the Potomac, facing off against General Robert E. Lee and the Confederate Army of Northern Virginia. This was the primary theater of war, and Grant knew that breaking Lee's army was essential to achieving victory. The resulting series of battles, known collectively as the Overland Campaign, would be some of the most grueling and bloody of the entire war.

The Overland Campaign began in early May 1864 with the Battle of the Wilderness. The dense forests and tangled underbrush of the Wilderness made it a nightmarish battlefield. Visibility was limited, and the thick woods caught fire during the fighting, adding to the chaos and horror. Grant's forces engaged Lee's in a brutal, inconclusive battle that resulted in heavy casualties on both sides. Despite the lack of a clear victory, Grant made a pivotal decision: instead of retreating as previous Union generals had done, he ordered his army to move southward, continuing the offensive.

This decision to keep pressing forward, rather than falling back to regroup, was a defining moment in the campaign. It demonstrated Grant's resolve and his understanding that relentless pressure was necessary to wear down the Confederate forces. Lee, accustomed to Union generals withdrawing after a tough fight, was now forced to respond to Grant's unyielding advance.

Following the Battle of the Wilderness, the Union and Confederate armies clashed again at Spotsylvania Court House. The fighting here was characterized by intense and often hand-to-hand combat, with neither side able to gain a decisive advantage. One of the most notable episodes of the battle was the struggle for the "Bloody Angle," a section of the Confederate defenses that saw relentless assaults and staggering casualties. Despite the horrific losses, Grant's persistence in maintaining the offensive pressure kept Lee's forces on the defensive.

As the campaign continued, Grant's strategic vision became increasingly evident. He aimed to grind down Lee's army through continuous engagement, knowing that the Union could replace its losses more easily than the Confederacy. This approach, often referred to as a war of attrition, was brutal but effective. The Union's superior numbers and resources would eventually overwhelm the Confederate forces if Grant could keep the pressure on.

CHAPTER 5: COMMANDING GENERAL

The next major engagement was the Battle of Cold Harbor, a name that would become synonymous with tragedy and bloodshed. In early June 1864, Grant ordered a series of frontal assaults against well-entrenched Confederate positions. The attacks were repelled with devastating losses, and the battle is often cited as one of Grant's few major tactical mistakes. The staggering casualties—many of them suffered in a matter of minutes—shocked the Union army and the public. Yet, even in the face of such a setback, Grant remained committed to his overall strategy.

After Cold Harbor, Grant shifted his focus to Petersburg, Virginia, a vital rail hub and supply center for the Confederate capital of Richmond. Rather than a single, decisive battle, the Siege of Petersburg became a prolonged campaign, lasting from June 1864 to April 1865. Grant's forces encircled the city, digging trenches and constructing fortifications in what became a precursor to the trench warfare of World War I. The siege was characterized by a grinding war of attrition, with both sides suffering heavy casualties and enduring harsh conditions.

Grant's strategy during the siege was to cut off Petersburg's supply lines and force the Confederates to defend an ever-shrinking perimeter. The Union forces conducted several assaults and maneuvers, including the infamous Battle of the Crater in July 1864. In an attempt to break the stalemate, Union engineers dug a tunnel beneath the Confederate lines and detonated a massive explosion, creating a huge crater. However, poor execution of the follow-up assault turned what could have been a breakthrough into a disaster, with Union troops trapped in the crater and subjected to intense Confederate fire.

Despite the setbacks and heavy losses, Grant's relentless pressure was taking its toll on the Confederate forces. The prolonged siege strained Confederate resources and morale, and the Union's numerical and logistical advantages began to tip the balance. Meanwhile, in the Western Theater, Major General William Tecumseh Sherman's campaign in Georgia further weakened the Confederate war effort. Sherman's capture of Atlanta in September 1864 and his subsequent March to the Sea devastated the Southern heartland, disrupting supply lines and breaking the Confederacy's will to fight.

As winter turned to spring in 1865, the situation for the Confederacy became increasingly dire. Lee's army, stretched thin and struggling to defend both Petersburg and Richmond, was running out of options. Grant's forces, bolstered by reinforcements and continuous resupply, maintained the pressure. In early April 1865, the Union army launched a final series of assaults, breaking through the Confederate defenses and forcing Lee to evacuate Petersburg and Richmond.

The fall of Petersburg and Richmond marked the beginning of the end for the Confederacy. Lee's army, attempting to retreat and regroup, was pursued relentlessly by Grant's forces. The Union's superior numbers and coordination left the Confederates with little room to maneuver. On April 9, 1865, Lee and Grant met at Appomattox Court House, where Lee formally surrendered his army. Grant's terms were generous, reflecting his desire for reconciliation and healing. The surrender at Appomattox effectively ended the Civil War, with remaining Confederate forces surrendering shortly thereafter.

Grant's leadership as Commanding General was characterized by his strategic vision, relentless determination, and ability to coordinate complex military operations across multiple theaters. His understanding of the broader strategic picture and his willingness to take risks were crucial in achieving Union victory. Grant's ability to inspire and lead his troops, even in the face of severe hardships and setbacks, demonstrated his exceptional qualities as a military leader.

The end of the Civil War brought relief and celebration across the Union, but the challenges of reconstruction and healing were just beginning. Grant's role in these post-war efforts would be pivotal, as he transitioned from military leader to political figure. His experiences during the war, particularly his commitment to Union and his empathy for the common soldier, would shape

CHAPTER 5: COMMANDING GENERAL

his approach to leadership in the years to come.

Reflecting on Grant's tenure as Commanding General, one can see a leader who understood the harsh realities of war and the importance of strategic vision. His ability to maintain focus and pressure on the Confederate forces, despite significant challenges, was key to the Union's success. Grant's legacy as a military leader is one of resilience, determination, and an unwavering commitment to victory. These qualities would continue to define him as he took on new roles in the post-war period, shaping the future of the United States.

Chapter 6: The Road to Appomattox

With the fall of Petersburg and Richmond in April 1865, the end of the Civil War was within sight. Ulysses S. Grant, now firmly established as the Union's top general, had pursued a relentless strategy that brought Confederate General Robert E. Lee to the brink of defeat. Yet, the final chapter of this epic struggle was to be written on the road to Appomattox Court House, where the decisive moment of surrender would take place.

As the Confederate capital of Richmond fell, Lee knew that his situation was dire. His once formidable Army of Northern Virginia was severely depleted, both in numbers and supplies. Despite the grim reality, Lee was determined to fight on, hoping to link up with other Confederate forces in North Carolina. However, Grant was equally determined to prevent this and end the war once and for all.

Grant's strategy in the final weeks of the war was marked by relentless pursuit and coordination among his forces. He understood that allowing Lee's army to escape and regroup would prolong the conflict, leading to more unnecessary bloodshed. Grant's orders to his commanders were clear: maintain constant pressure on Lee's retreating forces and cut off any possible routes of escape.

One of the key elements of Grant's plan was the use of cavalry to harass and delay Lee's movements. General Philip Sheridan, one of Grant's most trusted subordinates, played a crucial role in this effort. Sheridan's cavalry was highly mobile and aggressive, engaging Confederate forces at every opportunity and destroying supply depots. This constant harassment significantly slowed Lee's retreat and sapped the morale of his troops.

The Union forces' relentless pursuit reached a critical point at the Battle of Sailor's Creek on April 6, 1865. This engagement saw nearly a quarter of Lee's remaining army captured or killed. The battle was a devastating blow to the Confederates, further diminishing their ability to continue the fight. As Union forces closed in, the Confederates found themselves increasingly surrounded and outnumbered.

During these final days, Grant's leadership was characterized by a combination of strategic insight and a genuine desire to end the war with as little further bloodshed as possible. He maintained communication with Lee, offering terms of surrender that reflected his commitment to reconciliation rather than retribution. Grant's respect for Lee and his recognition of the need for national healing influenced his approach to these negotiations.

On April 7, 1865, Grant sent a letter to Lee suggesting that it was time to discuss terms of surrender. Grant's tone was respectful and straightforward, reflecting his desire to end the conflict honorably. Lee, understanding the futility of further resistance but still hoping to find a way to continue fighting, replied with inquiries about the terms Grant would offer.

Over the next two days, the correspondence continued. Grant's messages emphasized the need to avoid further bloodshed and hinted at generous terms for Lee's men. Meanwhile, Union forces were closing in, and the Confederate soldiers, exhausted and hungry, were losing hope. The pursuit culminated in the small village of Appomattox Court House, where the final confrontation would take place.

On the morning of April 9, 1865, Lee made the fateful decision to meet with Grant and discuss terms of surrender. The meeting was arranged at the home of Wilmer McLean, a peaceful setting that contrasted sharply with the turmoil of the preceding years. Grant arrived at the McLean house wearing a mud-splattered uniform, a reflection of his practical and unpretentious nature. Lee, ever the gentleman, was impeccably dressed in a full dress uniform.

The meeting between Grant and Lee was a historic moment, characterized by mutual respect and a shared desire to bring the war to a close. Grant's terms were simple and generous: Confederate soldiers would be paroled and allowed to return home with their personal possessions, horses, and sidearms. Officers would be allowed to keep their sidearms, horses, and personal baggage. There would be no trials for treason or other punitive actions. These terms reflected Grant's understanding that the nation needed to heal and that punitive measures would only deepen the wounds of division.

Lee accepted Grant's terms, and the formal surrender took place. The scene at Appomattox was solemn and poignant. Confederate soldiers, many of them tearful and deeply moved, stacked their arms and surrendered their flags. Grant's men, respectful of their former adversaries, refrained from celebrating or gloating. This dignified end to the conflict was a testament to Grant's leadership and his commitment to reconciliation.

The surrender at Appomattox marked the effective end of the Civil War, though some Confederate forces continued to resist for a few weeks longer. For Grant, the moment was one of mixed emotions. He was relieved that the war was finally over and proud of the role he had played in preserving the Union. At the same time, he was acutely aware of the immense suffering and loss that the war had caused. His thoughts turned to the daunting task of rebuilding the nation and healing the wounds that four years of conflict had inflicted.

In the days following the surrender, Grant focused on ensuring that the terms of the agreement were honored and that Confederate soldiers were treated with dignity and respect. He worked to facilitate their safe return home and to prevent acts of retribution. Grant's actions during this period demonstrated his commitment to fostering a spirit of reconciliation and unity.

The end of the Civil War was a turning point not only for the nation but also for Grant personally. He emerged from the conflict as a national hero, respected by both his soldiers and his former adversaries. His leadership had been instrumental in securing the Union's victory, and his vision for peace and reconciliation set the stage for his future role in American politics.

Grant's journey from a humble beginning in Ohio to the victorious general at Appomattox was marked by perseverance, strategic brilliance, and a deep sense of duty. His ability to learn from experience, adapt to changing circumstances, and lead with empathy and integrity were key factors in his success. As the country looked toward a new era of reconstruction and healing, Grant's leadership and vision would continue to shape the course of American history.

In reflecting on the road to Appomattox, one can see the culmination of Grant's growth as a leader and a strategist. His relentless pursuit of Lee, combined with his commitment to humane treatment of his adversaries, exemplified the qualities that made him one of America's greatest military leaders. The surrender at Appomattox was not just the end of a war; it was the beginning of a new chapter in the nation's history, one in which Grant would play a pivotal role.

The legacy of Appomattox is a testament to the power of leadership and the possibility of reconciliation. Grant's approach to ending the war, marked by respect and generosity, set a tone for the post-war period that emphasized healing and unity. As the nation moved forward, the lessons of Grant's leadership during this critical juncture would continue to resonate, offering guidance and inspiration for future generations.

Chapter 7: Post-War Challenges

The Civil War might have ended with the surrender at Appomattox, but for Ulysses S. Grant, the real work was just beginning. The nation was deeply scarred, and the wounds of conflict were far from healed. The post-war period presented a new set of challenges that required a different kind of leadership, and Grant was thrust into the forefront once more. His journey from military leader to peacetime advocate and eventual President of the United States was fraught with complexities and demands that tested his resilience and vision.

As the dust settled on the battlefields, the first priority for Grant and the Union leadership was to ensure a smooth transition from war to peace. The immediate task was to demobilize the vast armies, ensuring that soldiers returned to civilian life and that the transition did not destabilize the already fragile nation. This was easier said than done, given the vast numbers of troops and the logistical challenges involved. Grant's military acumen proved invaluable in organizing and overseeing this process, helping to avoid potential unrest and violence as soldiers laid down their arms.

Grant's approach to demobilization was marked by practicality and a deep empathy for the common soldier. He understood that many of these men had been away from home for years, enduring unimaginable hardships. His orders ensured that soldiers were treated with respect and that their transition back to civilian life was as smooth as possible. This involved providing transportation, ensuring timely payment of wages, and facilitating the return of personal belongings. Grant's attention to these details helped ease the process and demonstrated his continued commitment to those who had served under him.

However, the challenges of the post-war period extended far beyond the logistics of demobilization. The country was in the throes of Reconstruction, a turbulent and contentious process aimed at rebuilding the South and integrating millions of newly freed African Americans into American society. Grant, who had seen firsthand the horrors of slavery and the valor of African American soldiers during the war, was a staunch supporter of civil rights and equality.

One of the first significant steps in this direction was the establishment of the Freedmen's Bureau, an agency designed to assist formerly enslaved people transition to freedom. The Bureau provided food, housing, education, and legal assistance, playing a crucial role in the early years of Reconstruction. Grant supported these efforts, recognizing the importance of providing support and opportunities to African Americans as they sought to build new lives in the post-war South.

Despite these efforts, the path to equality was fraught with resistance and violence. The South was a powder keg of resentment and anger, with many white Southerners vehemently opposed to the changes brought by emancipation and Reconstruction. Groups like the Ku Klux Klan emerged, using terror and violence to undermine Reconstruction efforts and suppress the rights of African Americans. Grant was well aware of the dangers posed by such groups and supported federal intervention to protect African Americans and enforce the new laws of the land.

As Grant navigated these turbulent waters, his leadership style evolved. He was no longer just a general leading troops into battle; he was now a statesman dealing with complex political and social issues. This transition was not without its difficulties. Grant's straightforward, no-nonsense approach, which had served him well on the battlefield, sometimes clashed with the murky realities of politics. He had to learn to negotiate, build alliances, and deal with the often frustrating pace of legislative change.

In 1868, Grant's popularity and reputation as a war hero propelled him into the political arena. The Republican Party, recognizing his widespread appeal and commitment to Reconstruction, nominated him as their candidate for President. Grant's campaign was built on his military achievements and his promise to continue the work of rebuilding the nation. His slogan, "Let us have peace," resonated deeply with a country weary of conflict and eager for stability.

Grant's election as the 18th President of the United States marked the beginning of a new chapter in his life and in American history. His presidency was immediately faced with a host of challenges, including continuing Reconstruction, managing the economy, and dealing with the lingering effects of the war. One of Grant's first priorities was to combat the violence and intimidation tactics used by the Ku Klux Klan and other white supremacist groups. He supported and signed the Enforcement Acts, also known as the Ku Klux Klan Acts, which empowered the federal government to intervene in states where civil rights were being violated and to prosecute those involved in terrorist activities.

These efforts met with some success, but the challenges of Reconstruction were immense. The political landscape was deeply polarized, and Grant often found himself at odds with both radical Republicans, who demanded more stringent measures, and conservative Democrats, who opposed federal intervention. Despite these difficulties, Grant remained committed to the principles of equality and justice, though his presidency was also marked by significant controversies and scandals.

One of the most notorious scandals of Grant's presidency was the Whiskey Ring, a massive scheme involving government officials and distillers who conspired to defraud the federal government of millions in tax revenue.

The scandal implicated several of Grant's close associates, and while Grant himself was not personally involved, the affair tarnished his administration's reputation and highlighted issues of corruption and cronyism.

Grant's administration was also characterized by economic challenges, including the Panic of 1873, a financial crisis that triggered a severe economic depression. The panic was caused by a variety of factors, including railroad overexpansion and speculative investments. Grant's response to the crisis, which included efforts to stabilize the currency and reduce inflation, met with mixed success. The economic downturn had a profound impact on the country, exacerbating social tensions and contributing to the difficulties of Reconstruction.

Despite these setbacks, Grant's presidency saw significant achievements. He supported the Fifteenth Amendment, which granted African American men the right to vote, and continued to advocate for civil rights and equality. Grant also worked to improve the nation's infrastructure, supporting the construction of the transcontinental railroad and other public works projects that helped modernize the country.

As Grant's second term drew to a close, he faced mounting criticism and a growing weariness of his administration's scandals and controversies. In 1876, Grant chose not to seek a third term, stepping down from the presidency and retiring from public life. His departure marked the end of an era, but his impact on the nation continued to be felt.

In his post-presidential years, Grant embarked on a world tour, receiving accolades and honors from foreign leaders and experiencing firsthand the global influence of the United States. However, his later years were also marked by personal challenges, including financial difficulties and health issues. In 1884, Grant was diagnosed with throat cancer, a battle he faced with the same courage and determination that had defined his military career.

As his health deteriorated, Grant focused on writing his memoirs, determined to provide for his family and secure his legacy. His memoirs, completed just days before his death in 1885, were a critical and commercial success, providing a candid and compelling account of his life and the Civil War. They remain one of the most respected military autobiographies in American literature, offering valuable insights into Grant's character and experiences.

Grant's post-war challenges were a testament to his resilience and his commitment to the principles of equality and justice. His efforts to navigate the complexities of Reconstruction, combat violence and corruption, and rebuild the nation reflected his unwavering dedication to the country he had fought to preserve. While his presidency was far from perfect, his leadership during this tumultuous period helped shape the course of American history.

Reflecting on Grant's post-war journey, one can see a leader who faced immense challenges with determination and integrity. His commitment to civil rights and his efforts to bring about reconciliation and healing were central to his legacy. Grant's ability to adapt to new roles and navigate the complexities of peacetime leadership demonstrated his enduring qualities as a leader and a statesman.

As the nation moved forward, the lessons of Grant's leadership during the post-war period continued to resonate, offering guidance and inspiration for future generations. His legacy as a military hero, a champion of civil rights, and a steadfast leader in times of crisis remains an enduring testament to his contributions to the United States.

Chapter 8: Presidency

When Ulysses S. Grant was elected as the 18th President of the United States in 1868, he transitioned from the battlefield to the political arena, a move that would prove both rewarding and challenging. Grant's presidency was marked by his commitment to Reconstruction, civil rights, and efforts to stabilize and modernize the post-war nation. Despite his successes, his administration was also plagued by scandals and economic turmoil, which complicated his legacy.

Grant's election came at a time when the country was still reeling from the Civil War and deeply divided. His reputation as a war hero and his straightforward, no-nonsense demeanor made him an appealing candidate to many Americans who were tired of conflict and looking for strong, stable leadership. Grant's campaign slogan, "Let us have peace," resonated deeply with a nation weary of war.

One of Grant's primary goals as president was to protect the rights of African Americans and to ensure that the gains of Reconstruction were not rolled back. He was a firm supporter of the Fifteenth Amendment, which granted African American men the right to vote. This amendment was a significant milestone in the struggle for civil rights, and Grant worked tirelessly to enforce it.

Grant's administration took a strong stance against the Ku Klux Klan and other white supremacist groups that sought to undermine Reconstruction and intimidate African Americans. He supported and signed the Enforcement

Acts, also known as the Ku Klux Klan Acts, which gave the federal government the power to intervene in states where civil rights were being violated and to prosecute individuals involved in terrorist activities. These laws were instrumental in curbing the violence and intimidation tactics used by the Klan, although they did not eliminate these problems entirely.

Grant also focused on stabilizing the post-war economy and promoting national unity. His administration worked to reduce the national debt, which had ballooned during the war, and to stabilize the currency. Grant supported the implementation of a gold standard to combat inflation and bring stability to the economy. These efforts met with mixed results, and the Panic of 1873, a financial crisis triggered by overexpansion and speculative investments, posed significant challenges to his economic policies.

The Panic of 1873 led to a severe economic depression, which lasted for several years and caused widespread hardship. Businesses failed, banks collapsed, and unemployment soared. Grant's response to the crisis included efforts to stabilize the currency and reduce inflation, but these measures were not enough to fully mitigate the economic downturn. The depression exacerbated social tensions and contributed to the difficulties of Reconstruction.

Grant's presidency was also marked by significant achievements in infrastructure and modernization. He supported the completion of the transcontinental railroad, which connected the East and West coasts and facilitated commerce, travel, and communication. This monumental project symbolized the reunification and modernization of the country and played a crucial role in its economic development.

Despite these accomplishments, Grant's administration was marred by numerous scandals and instances of corruption. One of the most notorious was the Whiskey Ring, a scheme involving government officials and distillers who conspired to defraud the federal government of millions in tax revenue. The scandal implicated several of Grant's close associates, and although Grant himself was not directly involved, the affair tarnished his administration's reputation and highlighted issues of corruption and cronyism.

Another significant scandal was the Credit Mobilier affair, in which high-ranking officials were accused of accepting bribes in exchange for lucrative contracts related to the construction of the Union Pacific Railroad. This scandal further eroded public trust in the government and underscored the challenges Grant faced in managing his administration.

Grant's inability to prevent or effectively address these scandals reflected his lack of political experience and his tendency to trust his friends and associates too readily. His loyalty to those close to him, while admirable in some respects, often blinded him to their misconduct and undermined his efforts to promote good governance.

Despite these challenges, Grant remained committed to the principles of equality and justice throughout his presidency. He continued to advocate for civil rights and worked to protect the gains of Reconstruction. His efforts to combat white supremacist violence and support African American voting rights were significant steps forward, even if they were not entirely successful in overcoming the deeply entrenched racism of the time.

As Grant's second term drew to a close, he faced growing criticism and a desire for change among the American public. The scandals and economic difficulties that had plagued his administration took their toll, and Grant decided not to seek a third term. In 1876, he stepped down from the presidency, leaving behind a complex and often controversial legacy.

In the years following his presidency, Grant embarked on a world tour with his wife, Julia, receiving accolades and honors from foreign leaders and experiencing firsthand the global influence of the United States. This tour not only highlighted Grant's enduring popularity but also provided him with a broader perspective on international affairs and America's role in the world.

Grant's later years were marked by financial difficulties and health issues. He made several unsuccessful business investments, which left him nearly penniless. In 1884, he was diagnosed with throat cancer, a battle he faced with the same courage and determination that had characterized his military career.

Determined to provide for his family and secure his legacy, Grant focused on writing his memoirs. Despite his declining health, he worked tirelessly to complete them, and the result was a critically acclaimed and commercially successful account of his life and the Civil War. Grant's memoirs remain one of the most respected military autobiographies in American literature, offering valuable insights into his character and experiences.

Grant's presidency, with its mix of successes and failures, provides a nuanced view of his leadership and the challenges of governing a nation in the aftermath of a devastating civil war. His commitment to civil rights and his efforts to promote national unity were significant achievements, even if they were overshadowed by the scandals and economic difficulties that also marked his tenure.

Reflecting on Grant's time in office, one can see a leader who was deeply committed to the principles of equality and justice, but who also struggled with the complexities of political life. His presidency was a time of transition and transformation for the United States, as the nation sought to rebuild and redefine itself in the wake of the Civil War.

Grant's legacy as a president is a testament to his resilience and his dedication to the ideals of freedom and democracy. While his administration faced significant challenges and controversies, his efforts to promote civil rights and national unity laid the groundwork for future progress. Grant's ability to navigate the turbulent waters of post-war America, despite his lack of political experience, speaks to his strength of character and his unwavering commitment to the country he had fought to preserve.

CHAPTER 8: PRESIDENCY

In the end, Grant's presidency was a period of both triumph and tribulation, marked by significant achievements and notable failures. It was a time of great change and great challenges, and Grant's leadership during this period helped shape the course of American history. As we look back on his presidency, we see a leader who faced immense obstacles with determination and integrity, leaving behind a legacy that continues to influence and inspire.

Chapter 9: Later Years

After stepping down from the presidency in 1877, Ulysses S. Grant found himself entering a new phase of life—one that would be marked by a mix of global adventures, personal challenges, and a final act of literary triumph. Having spent years in the crucible of war and the tumult of politics, Grant now sought some semblance of peace and normalcy, though life had a few more twists and turns in store for him.

Grant's transition from the White House to private life was anything but mundane. Shortly after leaving office, he and his wife Julia embarked on a grand tour of the world. This journey, which began in May 1877, turned into a two-and-a-half-year odyssey that took the Grants to Europe, the Middle East, Asia, and beyond. Grant's tour was not just a leisurely vacation; it was a diplomatic mission of sorts, where he was received by kings, queens, and dignitaries as a representative of the United States.

The Grants' world tour was a testament to the global respect and admiration that Ulysses S. Grant commanded. Everywhere they went, from London to Tokyo, they were greeted with fanfare and honors. In England, Queen Victoria hosted them at Windsor Castle, and in France, they met with President MacMahon. Grant's visit to Japan was particularly significant, as he played a role in mediating a dispute between Japan and China, showcasing his diplomatic skills on the international stage.

During these travels, Grant had the opportunity to reflect on his life and the state of the world. The exposure to different cultures and political systems broadened his perspective and reinforced his belief in the principles of democracy and freedom. The tour was also a period of respite for Grant, providing a much-needed break from the political battles and controversies that had defined his presidency.

Upon returning to the United States in 1879, Grant was met with widespread acclaim. He was celebrated as a national hero, and there was even talk of him running for a third presidential term. However, Grant decided against re-entering the political arena, opting instead to enjoy his retirement. He settled in New York City, where he hoped to live a quiet life, away from the public eye.

Despite his intentions for a peaceful retirement, Grant's later years were far from serene. In 1880, he became involved in a business venture with his son, Buck, and a Wall Street financier named Ferdinand Ward. The firm, Grant & Ward, initially appeared to be a great success, promising substantial returns on investments. However, in 1884, the firm collapsed in a spectacular fashion, revealing that Ward had been running a Ponzi scheme. The scandal left Grant financially ruined and deeply humiliated.

The financial disaster was a severe blow to Grant, both materially and emotionally. Having lost nearly everything, he was forced to sell his beloved Civil War memorabilia and other personal items to pay off debts. The situation was made even more dire by Grant's deteriorating health. In 1884, he was diagnosed with throat cancer, a condition that would ultimately prove fatal.

Faced with financial ruin and a terminal illness, Grant demonstrated the resilience and determination that had characterized his entire life. He resolved to write his memoirs, not only to secure his family's financial future but also to set the record straight about his life and career. Mark Twain, a close friend and admirer of Grant, offered to publish the memoirs, ensuring that Grant would receive fair compensation.

Grant poured his heart and soul into his memoirs, working tirelessly despite his worsening condition. He wrote with a sense of urgency, knowing that time was not on his side. The result was a monumental work, "Personal Memoirs of Ulysses S. Grant," which provided a detailed and candid account of his life, the Civil War, and his presidency. Grant's writing was marked by clarity, honesty, and a lack of self-aggrandizement, qualities that resonated with readers and critics alike.

The memoirs were published posthumously in 1885 and were an immediate success, both critically and commercially. They secured Grant's family's financial future and solidified his legacy as one of America's greatest military leaders and a significant historical figure. The memoirs remain a classic in American literature, offering invaluable insights into the man behind the legend.

Grant's final days were spent at a cottage in Mount McGregor, New York, where he continued to work on his memoirs until he was physically unable to do so. Surrounded by his family, he faced his illness with remarkable courage and dignity. Grant passed away on July 23, 1885, at the age of 63. His death marked the end of an extraordinary life, one that had seen him rise from humble beginnings to the heights of military and political power.

The nation mourned the loss of Ulysses S. Grant. His funeral, held in New York City, was a grand affair attended by dignitaries, veterans, and ordinary citizens who came to pay their respects. The outpouring of grief and admiration was a testament to the profound impact Grant had on the country. He was laid to rest in what would become Grant's Tomb, a mausoleum in Riverside Park, New York, which remains a symbol of his enduring legacy.

Grant's later years, though marked by hardship and struggle, also highlighted his indomitable spirit and unwavering commitment to his principles. His ability to persevere in the face of adversity and his dedication to his family and his country are integral parts of his legacy. Even in his final act of writing his memoirs, Grant demonstrated the same qualities that had defined his life: resilience, determination, and an unshakeable sense of duty.

As we reflect on Grant's later years, we see a man who faced tremendous challenges with grace and fortitude. His financial misfortunes and health struggles could have easily overshadowed his achievements, but Grant refused to let them define him. Instead, he focused on what he could do to provide for his family and contribute to the historical record, leaving behind a lasting legacy that continues to inspire.

Grant's life after the presidency serves as a powerful reminder of the complexities and challenges that come with leadership and public service. It also underscores the importance of resilience and the ability to adapt to changing circumstances. Grant's unwavering commitment to his principles, even in the face of adversity, is a testament to his character and his enduring impact on American history.

In the end, Ulysses S. Grant's later years were a fitting conclusion to a life marked by extraordinary achievements and profound challenges. From the battlefields of the Civil War to the highest office in the land, and finally to his quiet work at a writing desk, Grant's journey was one of resilience, courage, and unwavering dedication. His legacy, preserved through his memoirs and the memories of those who knew him, continues to be a source of inspiration and a testament to the enduring power of perseverance and integrity.

Chapter 10: Legacy and Impact

Ulysses S. Grant's life, marked by extraordinary achievements and formidable challenges, leaves a legacy that continues to resonate in American history. From his pivotal role in the Civil War to his complex presidency and later life, Grant's impact on the nation is profound and multifaceted. As we reflect on his legacy, we see a figure whose contributions go beyond the battlefield and the political arena, influencing the broader narrative of American identity and values.

Grant's military legacy is perhaps the most well-known aspect of his life. His leadership during the Civil War was instrumental in the Union's victory, and his strategic acumen and relentless determination were key factors in the defeat of the Confederacy. Grant's ability to understand the broader context of warfare, coupled with his willingness to take calculated risks, set him apart from many of his contemporaries. His campaigns, especially the Vicksburg Campaign and the Overland Campaign, are studied in military academies around the world for their innovative tactics and strategic brilliance.

Grant's military leadership was characterized by a deep sense of duty and a commitment to his soldiers. He was known for his empathy towards his troops, often sharing in their hardships and ensuring they were well cared for. This rapport with his men earned him their loyalty and respect, and his straightforward, no-nonsense style of leadership inspired confidence and determination. Grant's approach to command, emphasizing discipline, resilience, and relentless pursuit of objectives, has influenced generations of military leaders.

Beyond his military achievements, Grant's presidency also left a lasting impact, though it was fraught with complexities and controversies. His administration's efforts to protect the rights of African Americans and enforce Reconstruction policies were significant steps forward in the struggle for civil rights. Grant's support for the Fifteenth Amendment, which granted African American men the right to vote, and his actions against the Ku Klux Klan were crucial in advancing the cause of equality and justice.

Despite the scandals that marred his presidency, Grant's commitment to civil rights and his efforts to combat white supremacist violence were notable achievements. His support for the Enforcement Acts, which empowered the federal government to intervene in states where civil rights were being violated, demonstrated his willingness to use federal authority to protect the rights of all citizens. These actions, while not entirely successful in eradicating racism and violence, laid important groundwork for future civil rights advancements.

Grant's legacy also includes his efforts to stabilize and modernize the post-war nation. His support for infrastructure projects, such as the transcontinental railroad, helped to connect the country and promote economic development. These initiatives were crucial in fostering national unity and encouraging growth in the rapidly expanding United States. Grant's presidency, with its mix of successes and failures, reflects the challenges of leading a nation through a period of significant transition and reconstruction.

One of the most enduring aspects of Grant's legacy is his personal character and resilience. Despite facing numerous personal and professional challenges, Grant remained steadfast in his commitment to his principles and responsibilities. His ability to persevere through adversity, whether on the battlefield, in the political arena, or in his later years facing financial ruin and terminal illness, is a testament to his strength of character. Grant's life story is one of determination, resilience, and an unwavering sense of duty, qualities that continue to inspire and resonate.

Grant's memoirs, written during his final battle with throat cancer, are a significant part of his legacy. "Personal Memoirs of Ulysses S. Grant" is widely regarded as one of the finest military autobiographies ever written. The memoirs provide a candid and detailed account of his life, offering insights into his thoughts and experiences. Grant's writing is marked by clarity, honesty, and a lack of self-aggrandizement, qualities that have endeared the memoirs to readers and historians alike. The success of his memoirs not only secured his family's financial future but also cemented his place in literary history.

Grant's influence extends beyond his lifetime, shaping the broader narrative of American history and identity. His efforts to preserve the Union and protect the rights of all citizens reflect the core values of democracy and equality that are central to the American ethos. Grant's legacy is a reminder of the ongoing struggle for these values and the importance of leadership that is committed to justice and equality.

In popular culture, Grant's legacy has been the subject of various interpretations, reflecting the complexities of his life and career. He has been depicted in films, television shows, and literature, with portrayals ranging from the stoic military leader to the beleaguered president facing immense challenges. These depictions often highlight the duality of Grant's legacy, showcasing both his significant achievements and the controversies that marked his presidency.

Grant's impact on American history is also evident in the numerous memorials and monuments dedicated to his memory. Grant's Tomb in New York City is one of the most prominent, serving as a symbol of his enduring legacy and a place of reflection for those who seek to understand his contributions to the nation. Other statues and memorials across the country honor his military achievements and his role in preserving the Union.

CHAPTER 10: LEGACY AND IMPACT

Educational institutions and military academies continue to study Grant's life and career, analyzing his strategies and leadership style. His approach to command, with its emphasis on resilience, strategic vision, and empathy towards his troops, remains relevant and influential. Grant's legacy as a military leader and a statesman provides valuable lessons for those who seek to understand the complexities of leadership and the challenges of governance.

In reflecting on Ulysses S. Grant's legacy, we see a figure whose life was marked by extraordinary achievements and formidable challenges. His contributions to the Union's victory in the Civil War, his efforts to protect civil rights and promote national unity, and his personal resilience in the face of adversity all define his enduring impact on American history. Grant's legacy is a testament to the power of determination, the importance of principled leadership, and the enduring struggle for justice and equality.

As we consider Grant's life and legacy, it is clear that his impact extends far beyond his time. His leadership during one of the most tumultuous periods in American history, his commitment to civil rights, and his personal resilience continue to inspire and resonate. Grant's story is one of perseverance and dedication, reminding us of the enduring values that define the American spirit. His legacy, preserved through his memoirs, memorials, and the ongoing study of his life and career, remains a significant and influential part of the American narrative.

Grant's legacy is complex and multifaceted, reflecting the challenges and triumphs of his life. From the battlefields of the Civil War to the halls of the White House, and from financial ruin to literary success, Grant's journey is a powerful testament to the enduring power of resilience, leadership, and an unwavering commitment to one's principles. His legacy continues to inspire and influence, reminding us of the enduring values that define the American experience and the ongoing struggle for justice and equality.

Conclusion: Reflections on Ulysses S. Grant's Journey

As we come to the end of our exploration of Ulysses S. Grant's life, it's clear that his journey was anything but ordinary. From his humble beginnings in Ohio to his final resting place in New York, Grant's life was marked by a series of extraordinary events and challenges that he faced with determination and resilience. As we reflect on his legacy, we find a man whose impact on American history is both profound and enduring.

Grant's life story is a testament to the power of perseverance. He was not an immediate standout at West Point, nor did he rise swiftly through the ranks of the military. His early career was filled with struggles, including financial hardships and bouts of depression. Yet, despite these obstacles, Grant never gave up. His persistence and dedication eventually led him to command the Union Army, where he played a crucial role in securing victory in the Civil War. This resilience is a key part of what makes Grant's story so compelling and inspirational.

One of the most striking aspects of Grant's life is his ability to adapt to changing circumstances. Whether he was leading troops into battle or navigating the complex landscape of post-war politics, Grant showed an impressive capacity for learning and growth. His tenure as president, while marked by significant challenges, also demonstrated his commitment to the principles of justice and equality. Despite the scandals that plagued his administration, Grant's efforts to protect the rights of African Americans and promote national unity were significant achievements that should not be overlooked.

Grant's memoirs, written during his final battle with throat cancer, offer a unique insight into his character and experiences. These memoirs, considered one of the finest works of military autobiography, reflect Grant's clear and honest narrative style. They provide a window into his thoughts and feelings, revealing a man who was both humble and deeply committed to his country. Grant's ability to complete his memoirs under such difficult circumstances is a testament to his determination and work ethic.

In considering Grant's legacy, it's important to recognize the breadth of his impact. His military strategies are still studied in military academies around the world, and his leadership during the Civil War set a standard for future generations. As president, his efforts to protect civil rights and stabilize the post-war nation, despite the significant challenges he faced, were pivotal in shaping the course of American history.

Moreover, Grant's personal qualities—his humility, honesty, and dedication—have left a lasting impression. He was a leader who led by example, demonstrating that true leadership involves not just strategic acumen but also empathy and integrity. His rapport with his soldiers and his commitment to their well-being were key factors in his success as a military leader. These qualities are as relevant today as they were in Grant's time, offering valuable lessons for contemporary leaders in all fields.

Grant's life also serves as a reminder of the complexities and contradictions that often accompany leadership. His presidency, for example, was a mix of significant achievements and notable failures. The scandals that marred his administration highlight the challenges of governance and the difficulties of maintaining integrity in the face of corruption. Yet, despite these challenges,

Grant's commitment to his principles and his efforts to promote justice and equality stand out as defining aspects of his legacy.

As we look back on Grant's life, we see a man who was deeply human, with all the strengths and flaws that entails. He faced tremendous personal and professional challenges, yet he approached each with a sense of duty and resilience. Grant's ability to overcome adversity and remain committed to his values is a powerful testament to his character.

In reflecting on Grant's journey, it's clear that his life offers valuable lessons for all of us. His story is one of perseverance, adaptability, and unwavering commitment to principles. Whether in moments of triumph or times of hardship, Grant's example serves as a reminder of the importance of resilience and integrity. His legacy continues to inspire and influence, reminding us that true greatness is often forged in the crucible of adversity.

Grant's impact on American history is undeniable, and his contributions continue to be felt today. From his role in preserving the Union to his efforts to promote civil rights, Grant's legacy is a testament to his dedication to the ideals of justice and equality. As we move forward, it's important to remember and honor the lessons of his life, using them to guide us in our own efforts to build a better and more just society.

In conclusion, Ulysses S. Grant's life was a remarkable journey marked by significant achievements and formidable challenges. His legacy is a powerful reminder of the enduring values of resilience, integrity, and commitment to justice. As we reflect on his life and contributions, we are reminded of the impact that one individual can have on the course of history. Grant's story is a testament to the power of perseverance and the importance of staying true to one's principles, no matter the obstacles. His legacy continues to inspire and influence, offering valuable lessons for future generations.

Printed in Great Britain
by Amazon